AUBE NA BING

A Pictorial History Of Michigan Indians

With Legends by
SIMON OTTO

Compiled By
M. T. BUSSEY

MICHIGAN INDIAN PRESS

The publication of this book has been made possible by grants from the Michigan Council for the Arts, Michigan Community Services Block Grant through the efforts of the Michigan Commission on Indian Affairs, Administration for Native Americans and the Peter Wege Foundation.

ABOUT THE COVER:

The three photographs on the cover represent the different eras of the book: 1865-1988. From top to bottom: a tintype from Hannahville Reservation, c. 1865, Peter Keshick Sr. Collection, Sara Teeple picking herbs, 1978, Win Awenen Nisitotung Collection, Sault Ste. Marie Tribe of Chippewa Indians, Jerry Pigeon holding his son Mark, 1988, Andre D'Artagnan Collection. AUBE NA BING is an Ojibwe word meaning "looking back." It seemed a fitting title for this book.

Contents

Acknowledgements i

Preface iii

1865-1920 A Passing Light —
   Wassemo Win Bimi Say 1

1920-1960 We Remember —
   Nina Wind Mik Wen Dana 35

1960-1980 We Are Watching —
   Nina Wind Nana Gato Wabme 67

Language Glossary 123

ISBN 0-9617707-1-6

Copyright © 1988, by the Michigan Indian Press, 45 Lexington, N.W., Grand Rapids, Michigan. All rights reserved. No portion of this book may be reproduced in any form without permission in writing from the publisher.

Printed by West Michigan Printing, Inc., 840 Ottawa Ave., N.W., Grand Rapids, Michigan.

ACKNOWLEDGEMENTS

On behalf of the Michigan Indian Press and the Grand Rapids Inter-Tribal Council, we wish to thank everyone who has helped with this publication. We especially want to thank our Council of Elders, our Advisory Committee and Wag Wheeler, for guidance and support. Credit is also due to Kayle Crampton, Sue Maturkanich and Evelyn Zeek for assistance with photography and to Kitt Dorsey for her designs and illustrations. We would like to thank Gordon Olson and Roger Henningsen for technical assistance and Howard Webkamigad and Mabel Shomin for language translation. Thanks to Susan Wiseheart for critical editing and a special thanks to George Cornell for assistance in reviewing the book. The encouragement and advice of the faculty of Kendall College of Art and Design is also acknowledged. Finally, we would like to express our sincere gratitude to the funding sources that made this book possible: Michigan Council for the Arts, Michigan Community Services Block Grant through the efforts of the Michigan Commission on Indian Affairs, Administration for Native Americans and the Peter Wege Foundation.

M. T. Bussey, Director
Michigan Indian Press

Illustrations and designs for the legends and title pages
by Kitt Dorsey.

PREFACE

The photographs included in this book span the time from 1865 to 1988. In bridging these years, we intend to reveal the cultural changes endured by the Michigan tribes. The adjustment made by the Ojibwe, Potawatomi, and Ottawa of Michigan was a heroic one. As our tribal lands were being taken by treaties, allowing limited room for hunting and food gathering, the Michigan tribes were faced with relocation, escape to Canada or acceptance of European farming methods and Christian teachings. Some were relocated on reservation lands in Kansas, while many chose to flee to Canada where they could continue to live in a traditional way. It is the group that chose to struggle and survive in Michigan that are poignantly revealed in this documentary.

The choice of photographs for this book largely depended upon the character shown in the pictorial image. This was the primary guideline in selection, among the many other aspects of Indian life in Michigan. We have attempted to explore the personality and uniqueness of the Anishnabek, from the time we were first photographed in the late 1800's to the present. Selections were also made of many photographs that have never been reproduced. In this way, we have tried to offer fresh views of the Anishnabek with the aid of these private collections.

Many ideas for this book were initiated by our first publication, *People Of The Three Fires*. After this publication, it became apparent that the impact and effect of the visual image was essential for complete presentation of the Michigan Indian experience. We began immediately to prepare a book that would concentrate on photography and be used as a teaching aid along with *People Of The Three Fires* in Michigan's classrooms.

We are pleased to print five legends by Simon Otto to accompany the photographs. These legends are very old, having been handed down for generations by storytellers of the Michigan tribes. They are an asset to the book and act as a complimentary facet to enhance the impact of the images. For many years, Simon Otto wrote an ongoing column for the Grand Traverse Record Eagle entitled "Native America Speaks." The legends included in this book were drawn from these writings.

Wherever possible, we have used the language of the Anishnabek to further impress upon the viewer and reader the unique culture of the Michigan tribes, who possess a rich and articulate expression. Please refer to the Language Glossary for complete translation.

We hope that the reader is inspired by the photographs and legends of this book to further investigate the cultures of the Ottawa, Ojibwe and Potawatomi. It is also our desire to continue to make available publications by and about Michigan Indians, presenting the unique perspective of the Anishnabek. At this time we are preparing an additional photographic documentary to include the many images not contained in this first book. We are also beginning a catalogued collection of Michigan Indian photographs. If you want to aid us in this endeavor, please send photos to: Michigan Indian Press, 45 Lexington, N.W., Grand Rapids, Michigan 49504.

1865-1920
A Passing Light
Wassemo Win Bimi Say

This photograph was taken from a tintype, c. 1865. The family is unknown, but believed to be from the Hannahville Reservation, where the photograph was found *Peter Keshick Sr. Collection.*

Marcus Otto, of Weidman, served in the Civil War, 1st Regiment, Michigan Sharp Shooters, Company K. He enlisted in 1861 and was discharged in 1864. He lost his right arm in the Battle Of The Wilderness, May 3, 1864. Photo was taken from a tintype, 1865. *Simon Otto Collection.*

Two young men from the Escanaba area, framed in an elaborate studio backdrop. Taken from a tintype, c. 1865. ***Peter Keshick Sr. Collection.***

This photograph, taken about 1868, shows the combination of traditional Anishnabe dress and European clothing. Notice the Ojibwe designs on the arm cuffs of the boy and the many necklaces worn by the woman. **Manistee-Ludington Indian Collection, Michigan Historical Collections, Bentley Historical Library, University of Michigan.**

A canoe pilot at the rapids near Sault Ste. Marie, c. 1871. *Judge Joseph H. Steere Room Collection, Bayliss Public Library.*

Three generations of Anishnabe women from western Michigan, c. 1885. *Andrew Wheaton Collection, Michigan Historical Collections, Bentley Historical Library, University of Michigan.*

This studio photograph of a young Ottawa woman from the Ludington area was taken about 1885. *Manistee-Ludington Indian Collection, Michigan Historical Collections, Bentley Historical Library, University of Michigan.*

A studio photograph of a young Anishnabe woman of the Muskegon region, c. 1888. *Manistee-Ludington Indian Collection, Michigan Historical Collections, Bentley Historical Library, University of Michigan.*

The family of Joe Pete of Beaver Island, c. 1890. Photograph taken at a temporary hunting camp on the island. Notice the basket makings at the bottom of the photo and the birch bark pieces held by the boy on the right. ***Beaver Island Historical Society Collection.***

Elizabeth Thorn, of Sugar Island, stirs food in a cast iron cooking pot, c. 1890. Called Sisibakwatominiss (Maple Sugar Island) by the Ojibwe, the island maintained a strong Anishnabe community. **Judge Joseph H. Steere Room Collection, Bayliss Public Library.**

A blueberry camp near Sault Ste. Marie, c. 1890. During the month of the blueberry moon (July), many Anishnabek made temporary camps and collected the berries for their winter supply. *Judge Joseph H. Steere Room Collection, Bayliss Public Library.*

A temporary camp wigwam, near Sault Ste. Marie, in the shape of a tee-pee, c. 1890. The structure displays a combination of birch bark and rush mats. Mats were often made of cattail rushes and placed inside the wigwam walls, acting as insulation in cold weather. *Judge Joseph H. Steere Room Collection, Bayliss Public Library.*

The combination of Anishnabe and Dutch cultures is seen in the clothing worn by these Ottawa women of western Michigan, c. 1890. *Manistee-Ludington Indian Collection, Michigan Historical Collections, Bentley Historical Library, University of Michigan.*

A Camp Hawk annual gathering, located near Hart at Cobmoosa, site of an old Anishnabe settlement in the early 1800's, c. 1882. *Lucille Pego Collection.*

My parttime destiny is to be a storyteller, like my father and grandfather before me. I am practicing an old custom, hoping that my sons will continue, if not them, perhaps a grandchild.

A gentle breeze from the west is blowing, soft white clouds, afloating in a never ending sea of blue. Just for a split second, Brother Sun's light is interrupted. I look up and see She-sheb, flying overhead. This is a sign to me, brought forth by She-sheb. It brings to mind a legend. I thank Brother Duck for recalling this story.

When Mother Earth was young and the days and nights were first created, everyone lived in harmony. All the animals talked and they were not enemies. They lived as one big happy family. Brother Sun would come up and provide warmth for the trees and plants to survive. When he went down, Grandfather Moon would take his turn and provide his light at night, but without warmth. This went on without fail night after night. Brother Sun and Grandfather Moon each taking turns, providing light for the animals.

As time went by, the moon began to mumble about how bright the sun was. Why couldn't he be bright too? Soon he went to Nanabooshoo with his complaint. "I am Grandfather Moon, I want some more light. Brother Sun shouldn't be brighter than I." Nanabooshoo told him, "This is what the Great Spirit wishes. You must be content." The moon, not wanting to question the Great Spirit's decision, backed off, but didn't forget.

Grandfather Moon decided to follow close to Brother Sun and try to steal some light and

warmth from him. Each day he would do this.

One day, Nanabooshoo saw the moon in broad daylight, high in the sky. He hollered, "Grandfather Moon, your turn is at night. Stay away from Brother Sun." However, the moon was determined to be as warm and as bright as Brother Sun, so he persisted.

Brother Sun, more than a bit disturbed about the moon, told Nanabooshoo, who said, "The Great Spirit will take care of it some way." So Brother Sun returned to his place in the sky, saying nothing to Grandfather Moon.

Grandfather Moon became furious because the sun would not complain or say anything bad about him. The moon said, "I'll fix him." He tried to get closer than ever to the sun, but the warmth was too hot. Many times he tried, each time pulling back. At last he thought, "I'll go up and stand still so that Brother Sun's warmth won't reach Mother Earth." As he did this, Mother Earth turned dark in the middle of the day. The moon laughed, "I've done it! I've done it! Now they can only see me."

What the moon didn't figure on was that Brother Sun became hotter and the moon couldn't bear the heat. He had to move on. That was the first eclipse of the sun. Ever since that day, the moon has tried to steal some of Brother Sun's warmth.

A gathering of the Honor Mission Indian Sunday School, c. 1895. *Manistee-Ludington Indian Collection, Michigan Historical Collections, Bentley Historical Library, University of Michigan.*

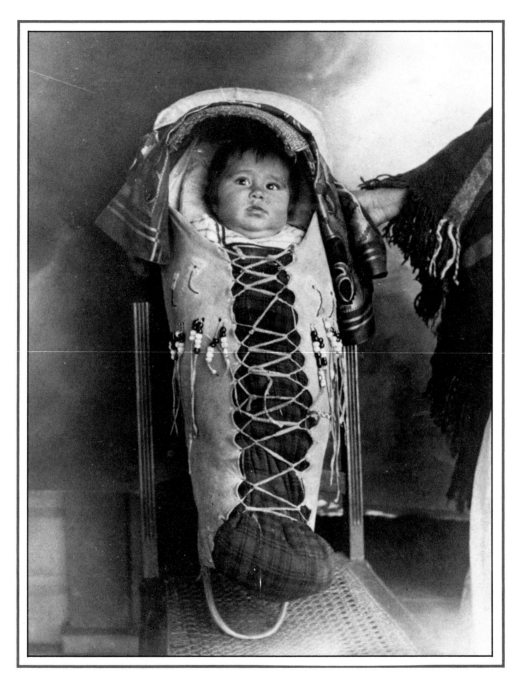

Ojibwe baby in traditional cradle board, c. 1900. Note the floral design and the beads stitched on the leather wrapped around the baby. *State Archives of Michigan.*

The Bird family of Peshawbestown, well known for their traditional baskets, quill boxes and quilts, c. 1904. *Edith Gilmore Collection.*

A view of logs, c. 1905, cut at Camp 9, Jackson and Tindel Lumber Company near Pellston, which employed many Anishnabe men in the region. Standing at far left, holding the horses is Henry Massey. Charles Massey stands center, atop the logs. ***Massey Photo Collection.***

The Mt. Pleasant Indian School football team, 1906, with brick dormitory buildings in the background. The school operated for forty years, from 1893 to 1933. *Simon Otto Collection.*

This photograph of Potawatomi women, from Dowagiac, was taken in Chicago where the women sold their baskets, 1909. *Alice Wesaw Collection.*

Netamop (Mrs. Joseph) of Sugar Island, holding Elmer Sprinkett, 1909. *Judge Joseph H. Steere Room Collection, Bayliss Public Library.*

The tailor class, Mt. Pleasant Indian School, 1909. Students learned basic academics, as well as vocational training in agriculture, home economics, carpentry, tailoring and welding. The boys in the front row of this photograph display the military cadet jackets worn by the students. **Simon Otto Collection.**

Three generations of Potawatomi men, displaying transitional stages of the people, c. 1910. *Roger Williams Collection.*

A Potawatomi camp gathering, 1910. *Roger Williams Collection.*

Mary (Mamie) Pine of Sugar Island, splitting black ash for basket making, c. 1912. She was born in 1887 and died in 1973 at Sault Ste. Marie. ***Judge Joseph H. Steere Room Collection, Bayliss Public Library.***

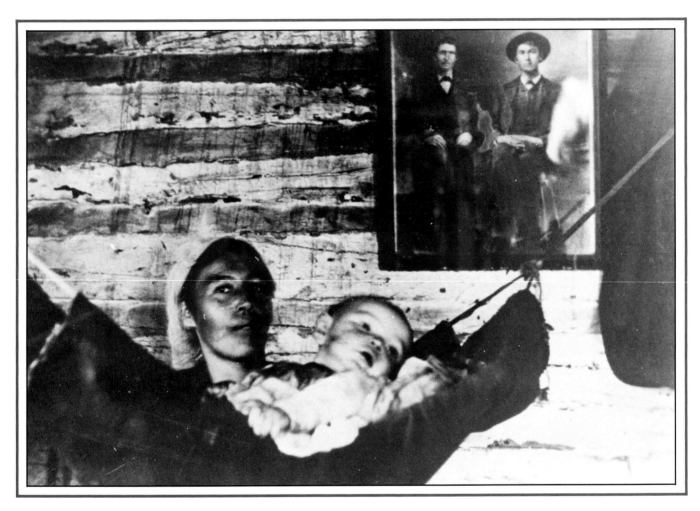
Mary (Mamie) Pine is seen behind a traditional rocking sling used for babies, c. 1912. The photograph in the background is believed to be her relatives. ***Judge Joseph H. Steere Room Collection, Bayliss Public Library.***

The practice of using cradle boards for infants was carried on in Michigan Indian communities until the 1940's. Today they are being used again by many who continue traditional ways. The young mother pictured here is Charlotte Gawgun with her child, Moline, of Sault Ste. Marie, c. 1915. ***Judge Joseph H. Steere Room Collection, Bayliss Public Library.***

The Chippewa Indian Baseball Club from Mt. Pleasant, 1916, one of many Anishnabe teams that played in Michigan from the early 1900's until World War II. *Lucille Pego Collection.*

Shortly after this photograph was taken in 1917, Elizabeth Pine, age three, died in a flu epidemic which killed many Anishnabek of the Upper Peninsula. ***Judge Joseph H. Steere Room Collection, Bayliss Public Library.***

This group photograph, c. 1919, was taken at Camp 6, Jackson and Tindel Lumber Company near Cross Village. At left, in the sleigh, is Henry Massey and at far right is Jerry Nishaw, both of Burt Lake. *Massey Photo Collection.*

A portrait of two friends from Cross Village, c. 1920. At right is Sam Leo. ***Massey Photo Collection.***

1920-1960
WE REMEMBER
NINA WIND MIK WEN DANA

A World War I Anishnabe soldier from western Michigan, c. 1920. **Manistee-Ludington Indian Collection, Michigan Historical Collections, Bentley Historical Library, University of Michigan.**

This photo, c. 1920, of the Gem Island cemetery on Memorial Day shows the grave of a decorated veteran. **Judge Joseph H. Steere Room Collection, Bayliss Public Library.**

John Blackman, a stone mason from Peshawbestown, c. 1921. Woman is unknown. ***Edith Gilmore Collection.***

At left, Mrs. Neff and her mother, of Burt Lake, c. 1921. ***Massey Photo Collection.***

Baseball team from Peshawbestown, c. 1922. From left, standing: Ed Blackman, Dan Chippewa, Dominic Chippewa, John Gingway, unknown. From left, sitting: Dennis McKee, unknown. **Edith Gilmore Collection.**

Moses Anse of Peshawbestown. Photograph taken, c. 1929. *Edith Gilmore Collection.*

Students at Holy Childhood Indian School, Harbor Springs, c. 1924. *Edith Gilmore Collection.*

The Simon and Harriet (Kosequat) Keway family, c. 1925. They are pictured here with most of their fifteen children and many grandchildren at their farm home near Good Hart. ***Keway Photo Collection.***

Two young men from Peshawbestown enjoying the Traverse City Fair, c. 1925. ***Edith Gilmore Collection.***

Long ago, when the Anishnabek were many, they lived along the waterways. There, many beautiful white birds of all sizes lived. The Anishnabek were friendly, feeding the birds and conversing with them.

One day, the fox, Waugoshance jokingly said to the birds, "I think I'll paint you different colors. I can't tell you apart." Most of the birds thought it was a good idea, all except Crow. Crow didn't want his clothes painted and he rebelled. He said, "Leave me alone. I like the way I am, so don't paint me." But, Waugoshance held the crow and started to paint him all over. "Now," Waugoshance told Crow, "you are too conceited, I'll paint you all over with black paint." Crow was raising such a fuss that he frightened the other birds and they flew away.

Now Crow was very angry over what Waugoshance did to him, painting his beautiful white feathers. "I'll get even with him for spoiling my feathers," he said.

Crow flew North and there he built a huge, long fence. This would keep the deer from the feeding grounds of Waugoshance. When Waugoshance and his friends went to the woods for deer, they found none. They sent the birds to look for the deer, but they returned without finding any.

Later, Kokoko was perched in a tree and she saw Crow coming. She quickly followed him and saw all the deer penned up behind a fence far away. She flew to Waugoshance and told him what Crow had done. Waugoshance hurried to Crow and said, "You are keeping the deer from us!" Crow laughed, "You turned my feathers black. Now you will turn black from starvation."

Waugoshance sent many animals to break open the fence, but each time, Crow beat them back with his wings. The wolves tried first, then a wild cat, but none of them could get past Crow. Waugoshance was puzzled. He then thought of his brother foxes. He sent two of them in to divert Crow's attention while another broke through the fence and freed the deer.

Crow was outsmarted. However, he felt satisfied with his vengeance and he told Waugoshance, "You painted my feathers black, you shouldn't have done that, but I've had my revenge by making you go hungry. From this time on, you will be able to kill all the deer you need, but leave the liver and the fat for me." Waugoshance agreed to do that, for as long as Crow lived.

So Crow turned out to be useful as a scavenger and to this day, you can see him along the roads, carrying out his duty that the first crow negotiated with Waugoshance.

Cora Shananaquit at age three, daughter of Albert Shananaquit of Mullet Lake, c. 1927. *Massey Photo Collection.*

A studio photograph from 1928. *Manistee-Ludington Indian Collection, Michigan Historical Collections, Bentley Historical Library, University of Michigan.*

Mt. Pleasant Indian School Marching Band, c. 1929. *State Archives of Michigan.*

The children of Lydia and John Lahey of Beaver Island, c. 1930. ***Beaver Island Historical Society Collection.***

Anishnabek turned farmers, taken on their farm near Mt. Pleasant, c. 1930. At left, Kenneth Gilmore, center, his sister and his father Ben Gilmore at right. ***Edith Gilmore Collection.***

The Louis Moses family of Cedarville, c. 1932. The men worked in the lumbering industry and the women were well known for their birch bark baskets. ***Massey Photo Collection.***

Ella Petoskey, seen here in traditional dress, c. 1934. She taught for many years at the Mt. Pleasant Indian School. *Florence Petoskey Collection.*

The cotton tail rabbit has a cousin who is much larger than he and who is protected by coloration. He changes colors from brown to white, according to the season; brown for spring, summer and fall and white for winter. He also is provided with larger hind feet, enabling him to walk on top of the snow. This is the reason that he is called the Snowshoe Rabbit. Now, he was not always able to change color. At one time, he was brown all year long, until a certain event occurred.

It was during the time when Earth Mother was in her infant stage and all animals could talk. It was the time when the first snow appeared and the cold came. It was the very first winter on Mother Earth.

A certain family of rabbits lived near a meadow bordering a swampland. They were a happy bunch, living in their snug nest. They had plenty of sweet clover and tender grass grew nearby. Their only enemy was the hawk, who had a hunger for rabbits. Their eyes were always skyward, watching for Brother Hawk. Their color hid them in the tall grasses and logs, blending with their surroundings. Brother Hawk often went hungry.

Then one day the weather began to change. The rabbits had never seen snow and they dug holes in the ground to shelter themselves. They had to adapt to living underground. They ventured out to feed in the meadow, but their food supply had turned brown and was no longer tender and tasty.

They started looking for food. They ran far from their nests and then Brother Hawk had the advantage. They were clearly seen in the white snow. Life was getting dangerous and hectic for them.

Finally, the rabbits said, "Let's ask Nanabooshoo." They scampered up to the hill of Na-

nabooshoo, ever watchful of Brother Hawk. They explained to Nanabooshoo what had happened; how their food supply had dwindled and how Brother Hawk was always near. Nanabooshoo told them, "You'll have to adjust to this situation."

So, the rabbits went home wondering how they could adjust. They pondered it over and decided to move their homes. They chose a hillside facing the swamp, because they figured if they wandered far from their burrow they could at least head for the swamp for cover.

Everything worked out fine for a time. They used the cover of the swamp as planned. They were content, even to the point of laughing at Hawk, because he couldn't catch them. The rabbits again went to Nanabooshoo, but this time they boasted about their good fortune. They even laughed about Brother Hawk being outsmarted. Nanabooshoo told them not to laugh at Hawk. They again laughed about it and Nanabooshoo cautioned them again.

One warm day the rabbits were out, far from their burrow. Brother Sun was shining brightly. The snow became sticky and the rabbits had to shake it off constantly. Brother Hawk saw them feeding and decided to sneak up on them. He swooped low to the ground. The rabbits saw him and ran quickly to the swamp. As they scampered, the snow stuck to their feet. They tried to run faster, but the snow kept building up on their feet. They tripped, falling over and over in the snow.

They thought the end was surely near. They lay very still, waiting for Hawk to pounce on them, but he flew on by.

They couldn't understand what had happened. They ran into the swamp and then noticed that the snow had stuck to their fur. They were all white and they blended in with the snow. That's why Hawk couldn't see them.

From that day on, every time they went out, they would roll in the snow, covering themselves. This became their new defense against Hawk. Nanabooshoo, hearing this told them, "From this day on, when the snow comes each year, you will turn white and live near the swamps." And so evolved the first Snowshoe Rabbit.

The baseball team from Holy Childhood School, Harbor Springs, c. 1935. This elementary school was opened in 1886 by the Franciscans to accommodate the Anishnabe children of the Harbor Springs region. *Grand Rapids Inter-Tribal Council Collection.*

Margaret Negake, a well-known basket maker at age 84. Photograph taken in Pentwater, 1939. *Lucille Pego Collection.*

Sophie Assineray of Good Hart, c. 1940. ***Native American Collection, Grand Rapids Public Library.***

Margaret Shawanibin attended Pellston High School when this photograph was taken in 1942. She is the daughter of Ben and Lena Shawanibin of Cross Village. ***Mabel Shomin Collection.***

Esther Massey displays some of her many baskets at her home in Pellston, c. 1945. Black ash and birch bark baskets were originally used by the Anishnabek for food gathering and storage. Later, baskets were sold to settlers and merchants as trade items. ***Massey Photo Collection.***

Rhinehart Wesaw played on the Dowagiac city baseball team when this photograph was taken in 1947. *Alice Wesaw Collection.*

Alice (Alexis) Wesaw with her two children, Sharon and Louis. This photograph was taken in 1947 at their home in Silver Creek, near Dowagiac. ***Alice Wesaw Collection.***

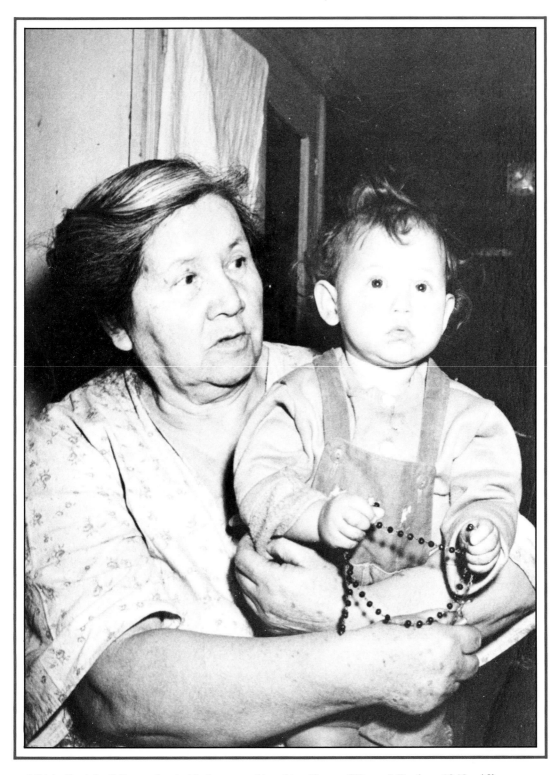

Libbie Baziel of Dowagiac holds her granddaughter Karen (Wesaw) Taylor, 1948. *Alice Wesaw Collection.*

Three generations of Anishnabe basket makers. Left, Sally Pego, center, Julia Lewis Alberts, right, Lucille Pego, 1951. *Lucille Pego Collection.*

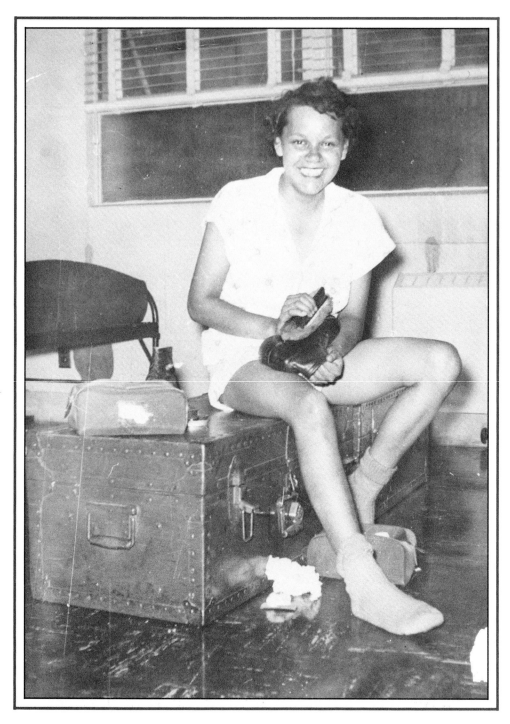

Josephine Cogswell, of Muskegon, joined the Woman's Army Corp in June, 1955. She served as a Specialist Clerk-Typist at Fort Jay, New Jersey. *Josephine Cogswell Collection.*

The Indian Cemetery at Iron River, c. 1956. From the early 1800's on, the Anishnabek made spirit houses to be placed over the graves. These spirit houses were used to honor and remember the dead. **Native American Collection, Grand Rapids Public Library.**

The Manda-Bee-Kee Dancers, an Anishnabe dance troupe from Petoskey, c. 1957. They toured Michigan in the late 1950's, giving demonstration dancing for schools and gatherings. *Simon Otto Collection.*

Weaving baskets at Bay Shore, c. 1958. *State Archives of Michigan.*

Carmeline Steele, winner of the Miss Indian Princess Pageant, 1960. The pageant was an annual event held in Petoskey for Anishnabe girls throughout the state. ***Simon Otto Collection.***

1960-1980
We Are Watching
Nina Wind Nana Gato Wabme

A studio portrait, taken in 1972, of Arlene (Petoskey) Naganasha and her daughter, of Petoskey. *Mabel Shomin Collection.*

Left, Lisa Bawden and center, Mike Shelafoe won first place for their 4th of July parade float of Anishnabe design, 1973. *Marquette Title IV Indian Education Collection.*

Phillip Chippewa, Jr. of Peshawbestown shakes hands with President Carter, 1977. *Edith Gilmore Collection.*

Sara Teeple, an elder of the Sault Ste. Marie Tribe, picking herbs, c. 1978. Photographer: Leslie Gaskin. **Win Awenen Nisitotung Collection, Sault Ste. Marie Tribe of Chippewa Indians.**

Henry Lewis and his sister, Lucille Pego, of Hart, present a flag to drape the casket of William Negake, to Post Commander Lane Tate, c. 1978. William Negake was the first Oceana County soldier killed in World War II. He was bugler and barber of Company H., 339th Infantry. The V.F.W. post in Hart is named in his honor. *Lucille Pego Collection.*

Champions of 1978 YMCA All Indian Woman's Basketball Tournament, sponsored by the Native American Outreach Program. Left, Kayle Crampton, Sue Parkey, Anna Crampton, John Crampton, Lucy Jackson, Linell Crampton, and sitting, Darcy Crampton. Photographer: George Pamp. ***John Crampton Collection.***

Third place winners of the YMCA All Indian Men's Basketball Tournament, 1978. Left, back row, Claude O'Berry, Bill Harris, Hank Huff, John Badwound and Pat Sagataw. Left, front row, Cecil John, Cordell Crampton, John Crampton and Leo Jackson, Jr. Photographer: George Pamp. ***John Crampton Collection.***

Bucko Teeple of the Sault Ste. Marie Tribe, c. 1980. Photographer: Susan Matrious. **Win Awenen Nisitotung Collection, Sault Ste. Marie Tribe of Chippewa Indians.**

George Nolan with tobacco offering at the Reservation Ground Breaking Ceremony, Project I, at Sault Ste. Marie. Photograph taken in 1981. Photographer: Susan Matrious. **Win Awenen Nisitotung Collection, Sault Ste. Marie Tribe of Chippewa Indians.**

The Lansing Teach-In, a coordinated effort of Great Lakes Educators to rescue the Title IV Indian Education Tuition Reimbursement Program. Photograph taken in Lansing, 1981. Photographer: Bill Davies. **Win Awenen Nisitotung Collection, Sault Ste. Marie Tribe of Chippewa Indians.**

Bill Church, center, presides over the tree planting ceremony on the grounds of the state capitol, 1981. Photographer: Bill Davies. **Win Awenen Nisitotung Collection, Sault Ste. Marie Tribe of Chippewa Indians.**

Adel Easterday, a Title IV teacher in bead work, c. 1981. Photographer: Susan Matrious.
Win Awenen Nisitotung Collection, Sault Ste. Marie Tribe of Chippewa Indians.

Sault Ste. Marie Summer Pow Wow, 1982. Girls in the dance circle. Left, Laurie Hunter, Jessica Gurnoe, Jessica Bouschor and April Bouschor. ***Win Awenen Nisitotung Collection, Sault Ste. Marie Tribe of Chippewa Indians.***

Students from Parkview School, involved in maintenance of Chief Kawbawgan's grave site, c. 1982. Left, Nichole Mayo, Michelle Mayo, Stephanie Holt, Ryan Sweeney and Home School Coordinator, Patricia Bawden. ***Marquette Title IV Indian Education Collection.***

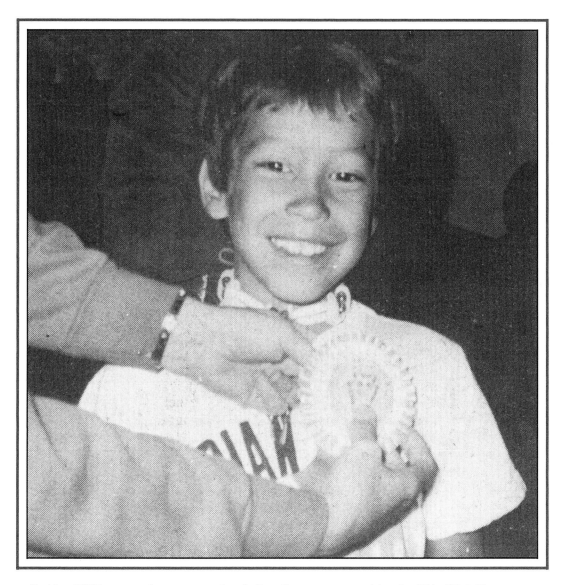

Sheldon Williams receives an award at Indian Camp, sponsored by the Title IV-A Program, 1982. *Marquette Title IV Indian Education Collection.*

Teaching sugar making to children at Sault Ste. Marie, c. 1984. The syrup is collected. Left, Carol Holt, right, Heather Simpson. Photographer: Susan Matrious. **Win Awenen Nisitotung Collection, Sault Ste. Marie Tribe of Chippewa Indians.**

Michael Holt stirs the syrup in a cast iron cooking pot, c. 1984. Photographer: Susan Matrious. **Win Awenen Nisitotung Collection, Sault Ste. Marie Tribe of Chippewa Indians.**

Pouring syrup into vat for boiling, c. 1984. Left, Edward Pine, right, Michael Pine. Photographer: Susan Matrious. **Win Awenen Nisitotung Collection, Sault Ste. Marie Tribe of Chippewa Indians.**

George Nolan is Santa for the children's Christmas program, 1985. ***Win Awenen Nisitotung Collection, Sault Ste. Marie Tribe of Chippewa Indians.***

Catherine Nertoli, with her daughter Luci Jo in cradle board which she made, displaying traditional floral design, 1985. ***Win Awenen Nisitotung Collection, Sault Ste. Marie Tribe of Chippewa Indians.***

Dancers at the annual Pow Wow at Mt. Pleasant, 1985. Photographer: Dorothy Reuter. ***Dorothy Reuter Collection.***

The Mite A Hockey Team of the Sault Tribe. Left standing, Bernard Bouschor, far right standing, Allan Bouschor, 1985. Photographer: Susan Matrious. **Win Awenen Nisitotung Collection, Sault Ste. Marie Tribe of Chippewa Indians.**

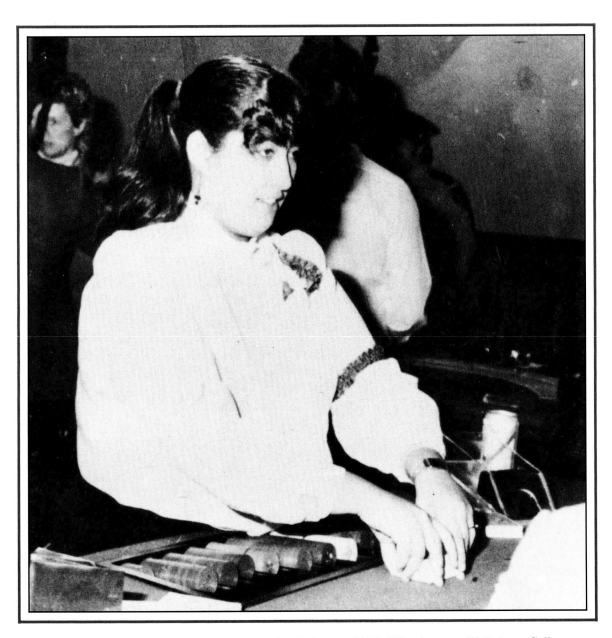

Reneé Robinson working at the Vegas Kewadin Casino, c. 1985. ***Win Awenen Nisitotung Collection, Sault Ste. Marie Tribe of Chippewa Indians.***

Conservation Officer Buddy Paul of the Grand Traverse Band of Ottawa and Chippewa Indians, 1986. Photographer: Jeremy Thomas Connolly. *Grand Rapids Inter-Tribal Council Collection.*

George Martin at the annual Grand Rapids Three Fires Pow Wow, 1986. Photographer: Jeremy Thomas Connolly. ***Grand Rapids Inter-Tribal Council Collection.***

A long time ago, the first man and woman and a little boy lived in a cave. The cave was dark and damp and sometimes filled with smoke from their fire. Then one day, First Man said to First Woman, "Come, let's go see how our forest friends live and how they build their houses."

The first one they came across was Eagle. His home was high on the mountain. Eagle said, "Look at my house, it is round like the sun and made of small logs, like branches." First Woman said, "You have a nice strong house, but it is too high for us." They thanked Eagle and gave him some beads for his hospitality.

As they went along, they saw Oriole's home. It was hanging down from the tree limbs. Oriole said, "It's a good home, see how strongly I have tied it to the branches. The wind can't blow it away." First Man said, "We can't live in the trees, but your home gives me an idea to weave some reeds together to carry things." They thanked Oriole and gave her some orange beads.

Then they heard a throbbing sound. They saw woodpecker, high in a tree. Little Boy shouted, "Where's your home?"

Woodpecker yelled back, "In a hole in a tree." Little Boy said, "We can't live in a tree, but make that sound for us again." Woodpecker made the sound on the tree. "Thank you," said Little Boy, "You've taught us

how to make the sound of the drum." They gave him some red beads.

Next, they saw Cliff Swallow on the wall, under a ledge. First Woman said, "Hello Cliff Swallow, show us how you build your home." Cliff Swallow flew down to the river and came back with some mud and quickly pushed it into place. "That's how I made my home." "Thank you," said First Woman, "When we build our home we could plaster it with mud." She gave him some black beads.

"We've seen how our brother and sister birds live," said First Woman. "Let's go see how the water people live."

They found Muskrat near a pond and asked him, "How did you make your home?" Muskrat said, "I made it of grass." "Well, it is a good home, but too near the water for us," said First Man. They gave him some fresh grass for his home.

Otter's home was in an old log, way back in the woods. Bushes grew all around her, and the stream was nearby. Otter said, "It's nice to live way back in the woods; it's cool and dark." First Man said, "It's nice, but we had a hard time finding you. We're afraid if we build our home in a place like this, we might lose it in the woods and never find it again." They thanked her and gave her salt for her dinner.

They heard a big splash and looked out on a pond and saw Beaver going to his home in the water. His home had a round roof and there was a hole in the top to let in the sunshine. First Woman said, "You have a good home and it has a good roof. We'll remember that when we build our home." They gave Beaver some beads and said, "Good-bye."

First Man said, "We have seen how the bird people and the water people live, now let's see how the insect people build their homes." They saw Caterpillar. Her home was a tent in the tree. Caterpillar said, "I make it from the silk string of my body." Little Boy said, "We have no silk string, so we can't make a home like that. Thank you." He gave her a comb for her hair.

Next they saw the spider's home in the ground. She was doing something. "What are you doing?" First Woman asked. "I'm weaving. I'm the best weaver in the world," said Spider. She then taught First Woman how to weave. "Thank you," said First Woman, "Now I can weave a mat for our door." She gave Spider some red berries to dye her yarn.

Then they saw Red Ant's home in the ground. It was on a small hill. "Come down the ladder," said Red Ant. They liked Red Ant's home, especially where the door was placed, facing the East, for the sun to shine in first thing in the new day. They thanked him and gave Red Ant some pretty stones for his doorway.

Satisfied now with all their brothers' and sisters' homes, they began to plan their own home. "It will be round, all the houses we visited have been of that shape," said First Woman. First Man agreed, "And the walls will be made of small logs, like Eagle's home and the roof will be dome shaped with a hole in the top like Beaver's home; to let the smoke out." "We will have a door facing the East like Red Ant's," smiled Little Boy, "So Brother Sun will shine in and awaken us." They agreed that Cliff Swallow's mud house was a good idea and that mud could be used to plaster between the logs. "And from Spider I learned to weave," said First Woman, "I can make a blanket for the doorway." "Oriole taught us how to make baskets, so we can gather berries and Woodpecker taught us how to make the drum sound, so we can call our people together," said First Man.

This is the way First Man and Woman learned to build their home. They were taught by their animal, insect and bird friends. Again, all was harmony on Mother Earth.

Fishermen of the Grand Traverse Band of Ottawa and Chippewa haul in nets aboard the Lady Hilma, 1986. Left to right, Junior Baldwin, Jerry Warren and Don Chippewa. Photographer: Jeremy Thomas Connolly. ***Grand Rapids Inter-Tribal Council Collection.***

Dave Trudeau displays the birch bark canoe he made in the traditional way with decorations of Anishnabe tribal design, 1987. Photographer: Catherine Nertoli. **Win Awenen Nisitotung Collection, Sault Ste. Marie Tribe of Chippewa Indians.**

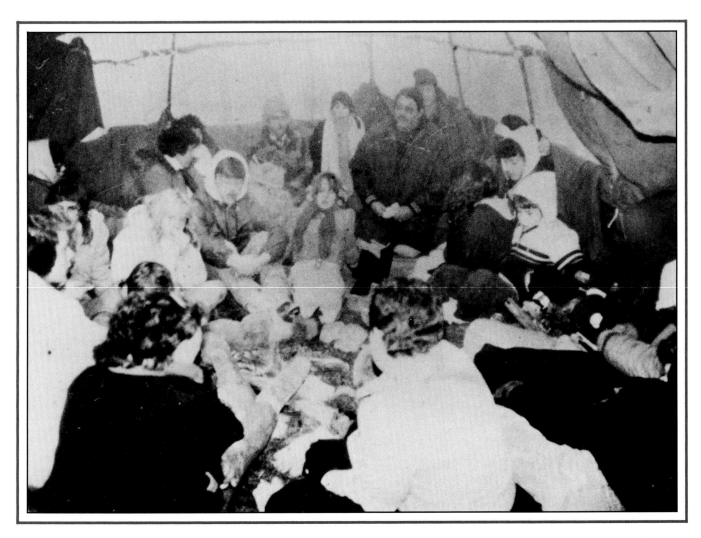
Smoke rises from a central campfire at a winter survival camp near Port Huron, sponsored by the American Indian Communities Leadership Council, 1987. *Port Huron Title IV Indian Education Collection.*

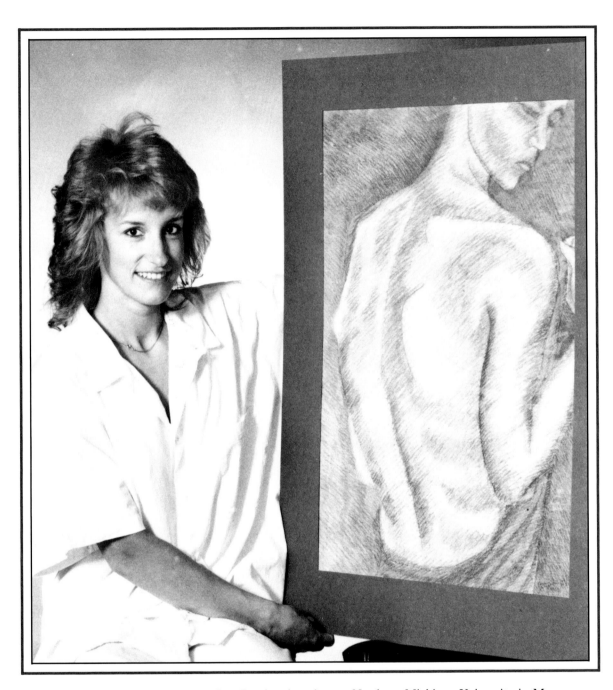

Lisa Conghlin, of the Keweenaw Bay Band and student at Northern Michigan University in Marquette, displays her drawing which was selected for exhibition in Yokaichi, Japan, a sister city to Marquette, Michigan, 1987. *Marquette Title IV Indian Education Collection.*

Girls dressed for the spring Pow Wow at Ah-Nab-Awen Park in Grand Rapids, 1987. Left, Carly Shananaquit and right, Arianne Memberto. Photographer: André D'Artagnan. ***André D'Artagnan Collection.***

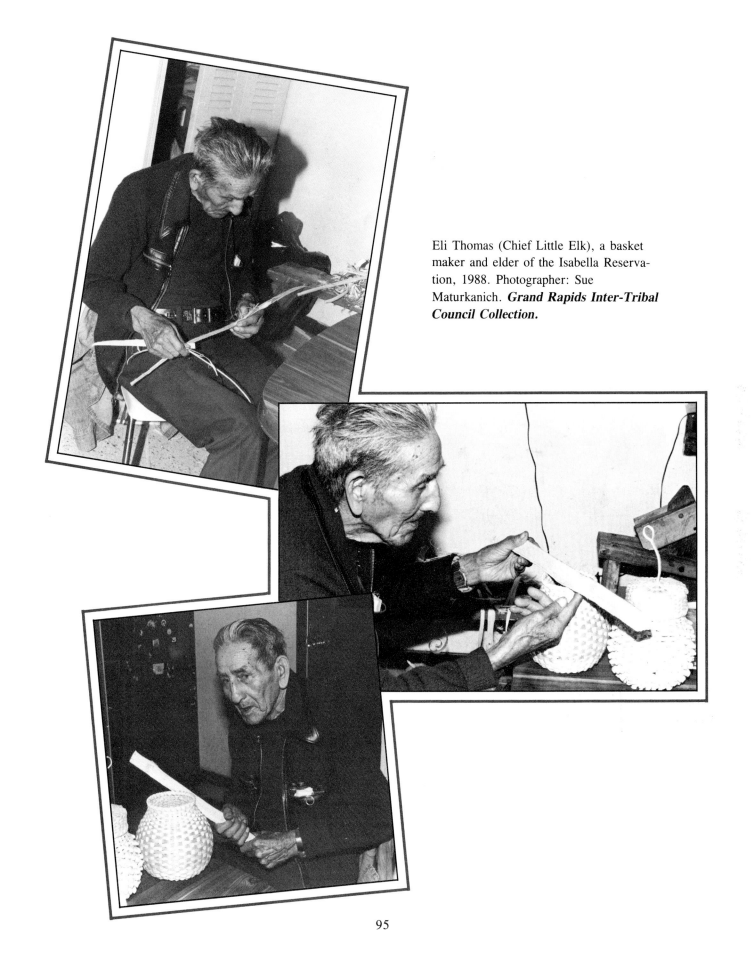

Eli Thomas (Chief Little Elk), a basket maker and elder of the Isabella Reservation, 1988. Photographer: Sue Maturkanich. **Grand Rapids Inter-Tribal Council Collection.**

The Two Hawk Singers, a traditional Anishnabe drum group, made up of men of the Three Fires Confederacy, 1988. Left, standing, David Shananaquit, Paul Raphael, Bill Memberto, Wally Hall and Jerry Pigeon. Left, front, Phil Memberto and Fred Raphael. Pat Naganasha is not pictured. **Grand Rapids Inter-Tribal Council Collection.**

Michelle Southerland reads with her grandmother, Alice Wesaw in Dowagiac, 1988. Photographer: Sue Maturkanich. ***Grand Rapids Inter-Tribal Council Collection.***

Spirit houses with stone grave marker in Indian cemetery at L'Anse Reservation, 1988. Photographer: Sue Maturkanich. ***Grand Rapids Inter-Tribal Council Collection.***

Sean Winters, a senior at Dowagiac High School, has been offered college golf scholarships to Notre Dame University and Middle Tennessee State University, 1988. Photographer: Sue Maturkanich. ***Grand Rapids Inter-Tribal Council Collection.***

Tasheena Raphael, daughter of Paul Raphael. Photograph taken in Peshawbestown, 1988. Photographer: Paul Raphael. *Grand Rapids Inter-Tribal Council Collection.*

Tom Anderson visits his grandmother, Charlotte Wayashe (right) and his great grandmother, Lucy Paul (left) at the Leelanau Memorial Nursing Home. Lucy Paul, at 105 years, is the oldest member of the Grand Traverse Band of Ottawa and Chippewa Indians, 1988. Photographer: Sue Maturkanich. ***Grand Rapids Inter-Tribal Council Collection.***

A team from the Summer Volleyball Camp at Bay Mills, 1988. Photographer: Sue Maturkanich. *Grand Rapids Inter-Tribal Council Collection.*

Members of the Keweenaw Bay Singers drum group, 1988. Left to right, John Paul Lakota, Neal Malmgren and Milton Bazinau, Jr. Photographer: Sue Maturkanich. *Grand Rapids Inter-Tribal Council Collection.*

Jerry Pigeon, with his son Mark, at the Native American Student Association Pow Wow, Lansing, 1988. Photographer: André D'Artagnan. ***André D'Artagnan Collection.***

Handmade baskets on display at the offices of the Potawatomi Indian Nation, Incorporated in Dowagiac, 1988. Left, Eli Bennett and right, Mike Denhoff. Photographer: Sue Maturkanich. ***Grand Rapids Inter-Tribal Council Collection.***

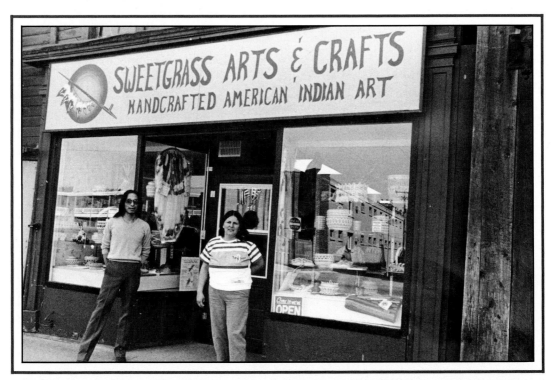

The Sweetgrass Arts and Crafts Shop in Sault Ste. Marie, 1988. Left, Brian Matrious and right, Maggie Krull. Photographer: Sue Maturkanich. ***Grand Rapids Inter-Tribal Council Collection.***

Julie Shagen, a junior at Sault Ste. Marie High School, 1988. Photographer: Sue Maturkanich. ***Grand Rapids Inter-Tribal Council Collection.***

Left, Quint Shawano and right, Larry Sprague, prepare a deer hide, Isabella Reservation, 1988. Photographer: Michelle Southerland. *Grand Rapids Inter-Tribal Council Collection.*

The Peshawbestown cemetery with Tasheena Raphael, at right, 1988. Photographer: Paul Raphael. ***Grand Rapids Inter-Tribal Council Collection.***

Albert Lothrop works as a fisherman at Bay Mills, 1988. He is the grandson of Albert "Big Abe" LeBlanc. Photographer: Sue Maturkanich. **Grand Rapids Inter-Tribal Council Collection.**

Jenny Little, of the Hannahville Indian School, holds a tobacco offering pouch which she made as part of the Sunrise Ceremony, 1988. This activity is designed to teach traditional culture and values. Photographer: Sue Maturkanich. *Grand Rapids Inter-Tribal Council Collection.*

The tobacco offering is carried to the central fire, 1988. Photographer: Michelle Southerland. *Grand Rapids Inter-Tribal Council Collection.*

Larry Matrious, left, a Resource Teacher for the Hannahville School, watches as students participate in the ceremony, 1988. Photographer: Sue Maturkanich. *Grand Rapids Inter-Tribal Council Collection.*

Neil Malmgren works on the sapling framework for a wigwam on the L'Anse Reservation, 1988. Photographer: Sue Maturkanich. ***Grand Rapids Inter-Tribal Council Collection.***

Carol S. Andary, a Chippewa-Ottawa Tribal Conservation Court Judge in proceedings at courtroom office, Bay Mills Reservation, 1988. Photographer: Sue Maturkanich. **Grand Rapids Inter-Tribal Council Collection.**

 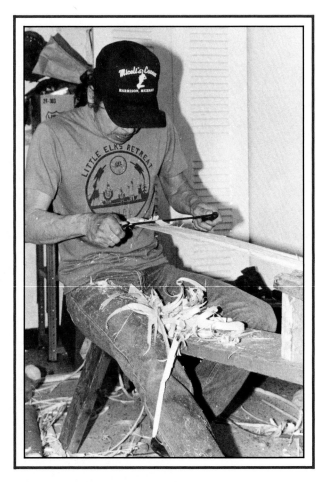

Larry Sprague making black ash baskets at his home on the Isabella Reservation, 1988. Photographer: Sue Maturkanich. ***Grand Rapids Inter-Tribal Council Collection.***

Elizabeth Pelto, of the L'Anse Reservation, enjoys breakfast in a Baraga restaurant, 1988. Photographer: Sue Maturkanich. ***Grand Rapids Inter-Tribal Council Collection.***

Keith Brant, manager of the Native American Gallery of Detroit, located in the David Whitney Building, 1988. Photographer: Sue Maturkanich. **Grand Rapids Inter-Tribal Council Collection.**

The Hannahville Indian School offers a unique program. Their primary goal is based on the traditional Anishnabe teaching of respect for the individual, through a holistic approach in academics and counseling. There are approximately 95 students enrolled, K-12, participating in regular curriculum as well as Ojibwe culture and language classes. The school has been in operation since 1975 and services the children of the Hannahville Reservation.

Bret Boda, showing his first grade reader, written and illustrated by the Hannahville Indian School, 1988. Photographer: Sue Maturkanich. ***Grand Rapids Inter-Tribal Council Collection.***

The Kindergarten Room of the Hannahville Indian School, 1988. Photographer: Michelle Southerland. ***Grand Rapids Inter-Tribal Council Collection.***

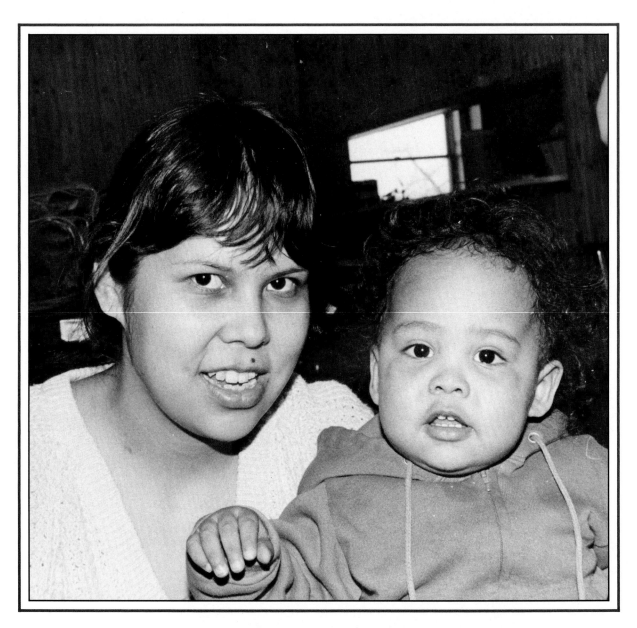

Carla Bennett and her son Eli at the meeting room of the Potawatomi Nation, Incorporated, Dowagiac, 1988. This new tribal facility was built in 1983 to accommodate members of the Pokagon Potawatomi Band. Photographer: Mike Denhoff. ***Grand Rapids Inter-Tribal Council Collection.***

Jo Ann Cook works in the Indian Art Store of the Grand Traverse Band of Ottawa and Chippewa Indians, 1988. Photographer: Sue Maturkanich. ***Grand Rapids Inter-Tribal Council Collection.***

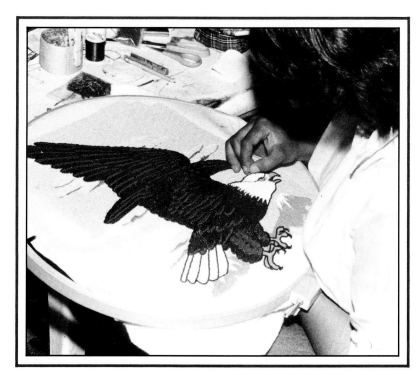

An example of fine beadwork from the Hannahville Reservation, 1988. The Anishnabek of Michigan used beads and bead-like objects for clothing and personal adornment for centuries before the arrival of the Europeans. The French traders brought with them mass produced glass beads, opening up new alternatives to traditional designs. Photographer: Sue Maturkanich. ***Grand Rapids Inter-Tribal Council Collection.***

Tony LeBlanc checks net for fishing, Bay Mills, 1988. Photographer: Sue Maturkanich. ***Grand Rapids Inter-Tribal Council Collection.***

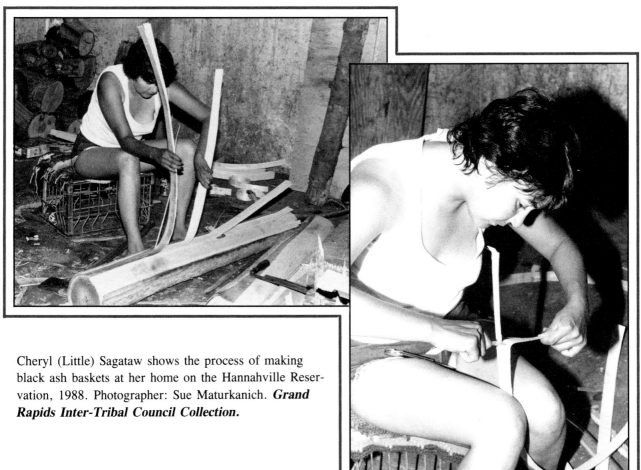

Cheryl (Little) Sagataw shows the process of making black ash baskets at her home on the Hannahville Reservation, 1988. Photographer: Sue Maturkanich. *Grand Rapids Inter-Tribal Council Collection.*

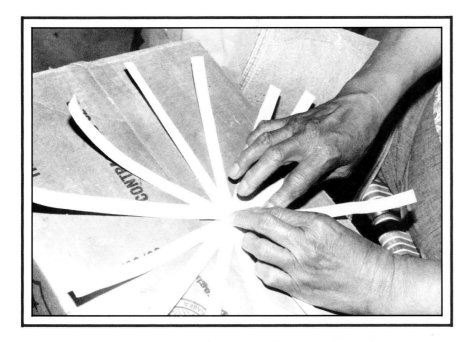

Hattie Little, of the Hannahville Reservation, begins shaping a black ash basket, 1988. Photographer: Sue Maturkanich. ***Grand Rapids Inter-Tribal Council Collection.***

The work in progress, 1988. Photographer: Sue Maturkanich. ***Grand Rapids Inter-Tribal Council Collection.***

Tonya and Terri Sprague at their home on the Isabella Reservation, 1988. Photographer: Sue Maturkanich. **Grand Rapids Inter-Tribal Council Collection.**

Language Glossary

PRONUNCIATION KEY:
A - as in father; E - as in bet; I - as in pit; O - as in boat; U - as in but.

Ah Nab Awen - the resting place.
Anishnabe - (singular) Indian.
Anishnabek - (plural) Indian, the original people, or the first people.
Aube-Na-Bing - looking back.
Cabmoosa - to walk about.
Chicago - skunk weed (wild onion or leek).
Chippewa - the name that the English gave to the Ojibwe people.
Kawbawgan - not sure, possibly from the Anishnabe word for raven or dipper.
Keweenaw - to carry a canoe.
Kokoko - owl.
Leelanau - the name of an Anishnabe woman that means the happiness of life or land.
Mackinac - not sure, possibly a blanket, Michillimackinac means big turtle.
Manda Bee Kee - water wonderland.
Manistee - the wind in the trees or forest.
Michigan - from mitchi gami, meaning great water or lake.
Mishomis - grandfather.
Muskegon - a swampy land.
Nanabooshoo - a hero and prankster with magical powers from Anishnabe legends.
Nina Wind Mik Wen Dana - we remember.
Nina Wind Nana Gato Wabme - we are watching.
Ojibwe - people of the puckered moccasin.
Ottawa - from Odawa, meaning those who trade.
Peshawbestown - from peswaba, meaning dawn.
Petoskey - the place of the rising sun.
Potawatomi - the keepers of the fire.
She-sheb - duck.
Sisibakwatominiss - Maple Sugar Island.
Waboose - rabbit.
Wasseya Bimi Say Win - a passing light.
Waugoshance - fox.
Wigwam - the dome shaped house made and used by the Anishnabek.
Win Awenen Nisitotung - he who understands.

BIBLIOGRAPHY

Baraga, Frederic. *A Dictionary of the Otchipwe Language*. Minneapolis: Ross and Haines, 1973.

Benton-Banai, Edward. *The Mishomis Book*. St. Paul: Indian Country Press, 1979.

Blackbird, Andrew J. *History of the Ottawa and Chippewa Indians of Michigan. A Grammar of their Language and Personal History of the Author*. Ypsilanti: Ypsilanti Job Printing House, 1887.

Cleland, Charles E. *A Brief History of Michigan Indians*. Lansing: Michigan History Division, Michigan Department of State, 1975.

Clifton, James A., Cornell, George L., McClurken, James M. *People Of The Three Fires*. Grand Rapids: Michigan Indian Press, 1986.

Densmore, Frances. *Chippewa Customs*. Washington, D.C.: Smithsonian Institution, Bureau of American Ethnology, Bulletin 86, 1929.

Dobson, Pamela J., ed. *The Tree That Never Dies: Oral History of the Michigan Indians*. Grand Rapids: Grand Rapids Public Library, 1978.

Edmunds, R. David. *The Potawatomi: Keepers of the Fire*. Norman: University of Oklahoma Press, 1978.

Fitting, James E. *The Archeology of Michigan*. Bloomfield Hills: Cranbrook Institute of Science, 1975.

Hamilton, Claude T. *Western Michigan History, Colonial Period*. Des Moines: Merchant's Life Insurance Company, 1940.

Hornbeck Tanner, Helen. *Atlas of Great Lakes Indian History*. Norman: University of Oklahoma Press, 1987.

McLuhan, T. C. *Touch the Earth*. New York: Promontory Press, 1971.

Reynolds, Charles R. *American Indian Portraits, From the Wanamaker Expedition, 1913*. Brattleboro: Stephen Greene Press, 1971.

Vogel, Virgil J. *Indian Names in Michigan*. Ann Arbor: The University of Michigan Press, 1986.